P9-EJJ-345

WITHDRAWN

21st
Century
Skills Library

ANIMAL INVADERS

BROWN TREESNAKE

Barbara A. Somervill

Cherry Lake Publishing
Ann Arbor, Michigan

CHERRY LAKE
Publishing

Published in the United States of America by Cherry Lake Publishing
Ann Arbor, MI
www.cherrylakepublishing.com

Content Adviser: Fred Kraus, PhD, Vertebrate Zoologist, Department of Natural
Sciences, Bishop Museum, Honolulu, Hawaii

Please note: Our map is as up-to-date as possible at the time of publication.

Photo Credits: Cover and pages 1, 4, and 8, ©USGS photo by G. Rodda; page 7, ©Photo
Resource Hawaii/Alamy; page 11, ©AfriPics.com/Alamy; page 13, ©Kenneth Vincent
Summers, used under license from Shutterstock, Inc.; page 17, ©Photographic Australia,
used under license from Shutterstock, Inc.; pages 19 and 22, Courtesy of F. Kraus,
Bishop Museum; page 20, ©AP Photos/US Fish and Wildlife Service/Gordon Roda;
page 25, ©AP Photo/USDA; page 27, ©AP Photo/Ronen Zilberman

Map by XNR Productions Inc.

Copyright ©2009 by Cherry Lake Publishing
All rights reserved. No part of this book may be reproduced or utilized in any
form or by any means without written permission from the publisher.

Library of Congress Cataloging-in-Publication Data
Somervill, Barbara A.
Brown treesnake / by Barbara A. Somervill.
   p. cm.—(Animal invaders)
Includes index.
ISBN-13: 978-1-60279-239-5
ISBN-10: 1-60279-239-9
1. Brown tree snake—Juvenile literature. I. Title. II. Series.
QL666.O636S66 2009
597.96'2—dc22   2008000801

Cherry Lake Publishing would like to acknowledge the work of
The Partnership for 21st Century Skills.
Please visit www.21stcenturyskills.org for more information.

TABLE OF CONTENTS

CHAPTER ONE

SNAKES!

A brown treesnake slithers in circles on Guam.

It is a typical weekday in the U.S. territory of Guam. The local school suddenly loses its electricity. Power losses are common on this small island in the Pacific Ocean. They can happen every few days. What causes them? Brown treesnakes!

Brown treesnakes climb up wooden power poles and along wires and cables. These power lines carry electricity from place to place. When a snake touches live and grounded wires at the same time, the power goes out.

These power losses, or blackouts, can affect a hospital, blocks of houses, or the entire island. Blackouts damage refrigerated goods, electrical equipment, and household appliances. They also disrupt businesses, government offices, and schools. Power losses cost Guam millions of dollars each year.

No one can stop the snakes from climbing power lines. All treesnakes feel safer off the ground. And to a snake, a

Learning & Innovation Skills

Invasive **species** are animals or plants not native to an area whose introduction harms the local environment, economy, or human health. The brown treesnake is one of hundreds of invasive species in the world. Do you know any other invasive species? Are there invasive species in your part of the country?

Learning & Innovation Skills

How did Guam's brown treesnake population increase so rapidly? Do the math. In this snake's native range, only one out of 10 **hatchlings** might reach adulthood. But on Guam, where young snakes find plenty of lizards to eat, as many as nine out of 10 hatchlings might reach adulthood. In some areas of Guam, the brown treesnake population has reached as high as 12,000 snakes per 1 square mile (2.6 square kilometers)!

power pole is not much different from a tree. So up the snake goes, finds the live wires, and zap! Another blackout occurs in Guam. The electric shock may kill the snake, but Guam has plenty more brown treesnakes—some say millions more!

Brown treesnakes (*Boiga irregularis*) do not belong on Guam. They first arrived about 60 years ago. No natural **predators** or diseases stopped the brown treesnake from spreading. In a few years, its population exploded and stretched across the island.

CHAPTER TWO

BROWN TREESNAKE LIFE

Brown treesnakes usually hunt for food at night.
This long treesnake climbs a tree in Guam.

Brown treesnakes are shy creatures. In their native range, they hole up in rotting logs or tree branches by day. At night, they hunt and do pretty much everything else. However, brown treesnakes in Guam have started to hunt during the day. This is because the animals that the snakes hunt at night have become scarce.

Many people say the brown treesnake's eyes look like those of a cat.

Brown treesnakes have light brown to olive skin. The snake's head is almost double its body width. Its snout is rounded. Its pupils are straight slits, much like the eyes of a cat.

In its native range, a brown treesnake grows to between 3 and 6.5 feet (1 to 2 meters) long. Brown treesnakes come from northern and eastern Australia, Papua New Guinea, eastern Indonesia, and the Solomon Islands. These areas have less food for the snakes and many more predators and **parasites** than Guam.

When the nighttime food started to dry up, snakes had little trouble switching to daytime hunting. Food on Guam is so plentiful that brown treesnakes often reach up to 10 feet (3 m) in length. Disease rarely strikes them, and few predators attack them. In Guam, a brown

21st Century Content

Brown treesnakes have thin bodies and are excellent climbers. They can enter buildings through windows, vents, plumbing pipes, and even narrow cracks in walls. They also slither through garbage in search of food. So most people in Guam snake-proof their homes. They keep their windows closed, and fill holes and cracks in house foundations and siding. They store pet foods in sealed containers and do not leave meat, soiled diapers, or open trash bags lying around. These precautions are a matter of health and safety.

treesnake might be more likely to die from electric shock than from being picked off by a predator!

Not much is known about how brown treesnakes breed. Females produce up to 12 eggs. Brown treesnake eggs are less than 2 inches (5 centimeters) long and leathery to the touch. Females may lay eggs two times a year.

The perfect brown treesnake nest is a hollow log, a crack in a rock, or some other shady site. The nest cannot be too dry or the eggs will shrivel up.

At about 15 inches (38 cm) long, hatchlings catch their own food right away. They feed and grow, and feed and grow. Young snakes eat small lizards and the occasional frog. As they get older, brown treesnakes add birds, bird eggs, larger lizards, chickens, small pets, and even human food to their diets. A backyard barbecue in Guam can turn into a spine-tingling event when brown treesnakes drop by for a burger!

Like this house snake, a treesnake constricts, or squeezes, its victim before eating it. The victim here is a lizard called a gecko.

Brown treesnakes are **semiconstrictors**. That means they use **venom** and squeeze to kill their victims.

But brown treesnakes aren't as great a danger to humans as cobras or rattlesnakes. They do not use front

21st Century Content

Brown treesnakes can bite humans, though it is only young victims who suffer. When a snake bites down on an infant's arm or leg, it does so repeatedly, pumping venom into the body. The venom is too weak to harm adults. But children with bites should be hospitalized immediately.

fangs to deliver venom. Instead, the delivery system involves the rear teeth and chewing the flesh. After catching its victim, a brown treesnake holds its meal in a tight squeeze while biting down repeatedly to deliver the venom. Then the snake eats its food in typical snake style—head first.

CHAPTER THREE

SNAKE INVADER

*Humans probably brought brown treesnakes to the
Pacific island of Guam in the 1940s.*

Brown treesnakes first came to Guam most likely as

stowaways in military cargo from Papua New Guinea.

U.S. shipments of war materials stopped at Guam on

Learning
&
Innovation
Skills

Guam is an island, and the brown treesnakes have no place to go— or do they? Ships pull into Agana and Apra harbors daily to load and unload cargo. Planes also leave the island daily. Do you think people are right to be worried about the snakes spreading to other places? How can people prevent the snakes from sneaking onto ships or planes?

the way to military bases soon after World War II ended in 1945. Once the snakes reached Guam, there was no stopping them.

The first brown treesnake sighting on Guam was in 1952 near Apra Harbor, a busy shipping center. By 1955, fewer than a dozen snakes had been reported. No one was particularly worried about the snakes' arrival on the island.

By the mid-1960s, the snakes had spread throughout the lower half of the island. By 1968, brown treesnakes were at the northern end of the island. Although no one knew or imagined it was a problem yet, brown treesnakes had taken over Guam.

Brown treesnakes spreading to other places is another problem. It doesn't help that Guam is a major western Pacific shipping hub. Air and sea traffic go daily from Guam to other islands, including Hawaii, as well as to mainland United States. Brown treesnakes hitch rides in shipping containers and even wheel wells of airplanes. Inspectors must take extra care to prevent the snakes from spreading elsewhere.

The greatest concern is in Hawaii. A brown treesnake is one tourist that is not welcome there. These animal invaders would threaten Hawaii's wide range of unusual birds and animals, many of which are threatened or **endangered**. They would also cost the state millions of dollars a year to deal with the blackouts.

But brown treesnakes have made their way to Hawaii. In 1981, a young brown treesnake was found in Honolulu's airport. A few months later, a second snake was found at

Naval Air Station Barbers Point. Over the years, several more snakes have been captured at Hickam Air Force Base.

Brown treesnakes usually come to Hawaii on military flights, but the snakes do not mind flying on regular airlines. In 1998, a dead snake fell from a jet after it landed in Oahu.

So far, it seems brown treesnakes have not made their way past Hawaii's airport inspectors. But it's important to continue the inspections. If the snakes get through, the islands will face the same problems that Guam has struggled with for the past 50 years.

CHAPTER FOUR

PROBLEMS, PROBLEMS, PROBLEMS

When they live where they belong, brown treesnakes are not a problem. This brown treesnake, with reddish coloring and large blotches, lives in its natural range of Australia.

Guam's alien invader is the cause of many problems. The brown treesnake damages the island's economy and inconveniences residents. It also introduces health risks. But perhaps the worst thing this snake does is destroy Guam's special environment.

Nearly all of Guam's native species with backbones, or **vertebrates**, have suffered because of brown treesnakes. With few native predators on the island, birds, bats, and lizards had little fear of attack. They do not naturally flee when a snake approaches. By the time an animal recognizes danger, it is already on the snake's menu.

The snakes have seriously damaged Guam's wildlife. Ten of 13 native forest birds, three of four seabirds, and six of 12 species of lizards have been completely wiped off Guam by the brown treesnake.

The introduction of brown treesnakes has caused other harmful effects. Birds, lizards, and bats feed on insects. And fewer of these animals mean more insects. As a result, diseases carried by insects, such as dengue fever, have increased.

Brown treesnakes have also damaged farming in Guam. Those additional insects harm fruit and vegetable crops. The brown treesnakes have destroyed chicken farming and

Brown treesnakes have found plenty of food sources on Guam.
They have also caused serious problems for the island's wildlife.

egg production. People pay more for eggs that must be shipped to the island.

Because of the brown treesnake, Guam's transportation costs have gone up. Checking every departing plane, ship, and cargo container for hidden snakes takes time and costs money. Also, tourism on the island has gone down, and government expenses have grown.

While visitors to Guam treasure the island's beautiful wildlife, they take no pleasure in brown treesnakes slithering through the grass.

With sunny weather, sandy beaches, and blue Pacific waters, Guam is a perfect tourist site. In fact, tourism is the island's second-largest industry, after military and government business. However, brown treesnakes do not keep to the forests. They sneak into hotels, restaurants, and shops. And that's not great for business.

Guam is a U.S. territory. The federal and territorial governments work together to oversee its natural resources. Brown treesnakes add costs to wildlife programs, including a plan to bring back species that have been lost to the island. One way to return a species to its native range is to breed the animals and release them into the wild.

Wildlife protection, educational programs, port inspectors, and the repair of electrical equipment damaged by the snakes cost millions of dollars every year. It's a steep price for an island with fewer than 200,000 residents.

Herpetologists study **reptiles** including snakes, frogs, and lizards—and **amphibians**, which includes frogs, toads, and salamanders. Most herpetologists work in universities, natural history museums, or game and wildlife agencies. Herpetologists usually have a master's or doctoral degree. The U.S. Geological Survey employs herpetologists to help deal with brown treesnakes on Guam. It is not a career for the squeamish—or for those who like to travel in comfort. Some herpetologists conduct their research on-site. That means camping for a time in deserts, swamps, or jungles.

CHAPTER FIVE

CURRENT EFFORTS

*Catching a quick-moving treesnake that comes
out mostly at night is a challenge.*

Before you can get rid of brown treesnakes, you first need
to find them. That's not such an easy task. Most of these
snakes hide during the day, and they are difficult to find at
night. It is also difficult to find their eggs, which they lay
anytime during the year. They produce young faster than
humans can remove them.

Current efforts to control the snakes include trapping, physical barriers, visual inspection, and detection dogs. Each effort has had some success. But the controls are costly and far from perfect.

Trapping requires designing, testing, and setting up snake traps. Over the years, scientists have tested almost 50 different designs and conducted more than 24,000 experiments. The most successful trap is a kind of funnel made of mesh. It can capture several snakes at once.

Each trap costs between $7 and $40. The trap uses live mice as bait to attract the snakes. Thousands of traps are needed to cover 1 square mile (2.6 sq km). Someone must check on the live bait and

Learning & Innovation Skills

Why don't Guam officials just poison the snakes? That is a simple question with a tricky answer. Snakes are not easy to poison. The snake's excellent sense of smell keeps it from eating tainted food. And because snakes don't eat every day, poisoned bait is more likely to kill the wrong species. What problems would that cause?

empty the traps regularly. From 1994 to 1998, Wildlife Services on Guam trapped more than 17,600 snakes. It is only a small fraction of the snakes living on the island.

Using physical barriers works much like trapping. Scientists and engineers have worked together to find a successful barrier to stop the snakes' movements. So far, they have tested vinyl, concrete, and hardware cloth barriers.

Brown treesnakes need very little rough surface to grip for climbing. Perfectly smooth vinyl works for a while. But then sun and wind roughen the vinyl surface and allow the snakes to climb. Concrete has the same problem. Hardware cloth is the cheapest of the barrier materials. It can be fitted onto chain-link fences, but the cloth only lasts years.

Barriers, like traps, are somewhat successful when used in specific locations. For example, builders set up a hardware cloth fence around the seaport of Rota in the

A brown treesnake is trapped at one of Guam's military bases.

Northern Mariana Islands to keep any arriving snakes from leaving the cargo area and reaching the city. The same type of barrier surrounds an area on Naval Base Guam that is a protected habitat for an endangered ground bird—the Guam rail.

Learning & Innovation Skills

Why doesn't Guam introduce a so-called top predator—such as a mongoose, kingsnake, or eagle—that hunts snakes? Japan tried introducing the mongoose to help with its snake and rat problems. Unfortunately, the mongooses also went after other animals. The experiment was a failure. Kingsnakes do eat other snakes, but they are ground snakes, not climbers like brown treesnakes. The only eagle that eats nothing but snakes is the short-toed bald eagle. That eagle species needs a huge forest to survive. Guam simply is not big enough.

The answer to an invasive species is never introducing another species. That action creates new problems and rarely works. Can you think of any other reasons why introducing top predators might be a bad idea?

Dogs make good snake catchers. Jack Russell terriers seem to be the most successful breed. Trainers teach the dogs how to cue in on or "smell" a snake. Teams of these detection dogs and their handlers patrol all cargo areas at the seaports and airports. However, the large, hot cargo areas are filled with strange scents and lots of noise. And it can sometimes be difficult for handlers to read the dogs' signs properly.

Scientists, engineers, and wildlife managers continue to look for solutions to Guam's snake problems. In the meantime, people have reported brown treesnakes on islands near Guam. Unlike on Guam, officials on

An inspector and her detection dog search for fruits, vegetables, and any sign of brown treesnakes among containers at Hawaii's Honolulu International Airport.

these islands put controls in place immediately. Perhaps continued research will discover the one thing that will remove all brown treesnakes from Guam. For now, we will have to settle for containing the spread of this animal invader.

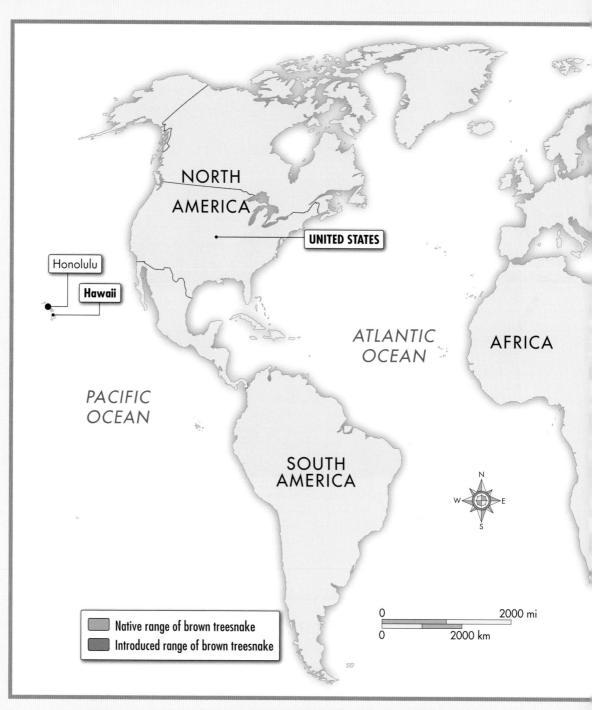

This map shows where in the world the brown treesnake

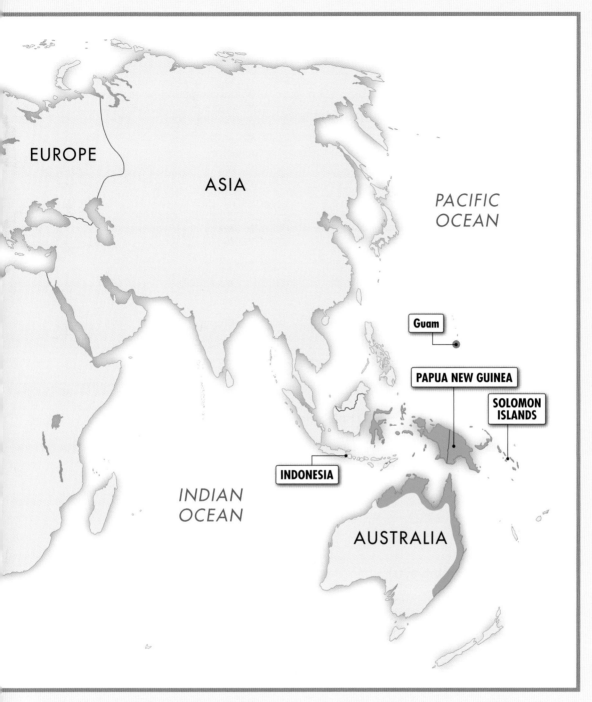

EUROPE

ASIA

PACIFIC
OCEAN

Guam

PAPUA NEW GUINEA

SOLOMON
ISLANDS

INDONESIA

INDIAN
OCEAN

AUSTRALIA

lives naturally and where it has invaded.

GLOSSARY

amphibians (am-FIB-ee-uhnz) cold-blooded animals with backbones and no scales or claws; frogs, toads, and salamanders are amphibians

endangered (en-DAYN-jurd) in danger of dying out completely

hatchlings (HATCH-lingz) newly hatched birds, amphibians, fish, or reptiles

herpetologists (her-puh-TOL-uh-jihsts) people who study reptiles and amphibians

parasites (PERH-uh-sites) animals or plants that live by feeding off, or living on or in, a host plant or animal

predators (PRED-uh-turz) animals that hunt other animals for food

reptiles (REP-tiles) cold-blooded animals covered with scales or horny plates that breathe with lungs; snakes, turtles, and crocodiles are reptiles

semiconstrictors (SEH-mee-kuhn-STRIKT-uhrz) snakes that use venom and squeeze to kill their victims

species (SPEE-sheez) a group of similar plants or animals

venom (VEN-uhm) poison produced and usually injected by some snakes, spiders, and other animals

vertebrates (VUHR-tuh-braytz) animals with backbones

FOR MORE INFORMATION

Books

Embacher, Eric. *Stowed Away*. Minneapolis: Tandem Library, 2004.

Fredericks, Anthony D. *Fearsome Fangs*. Danbury, CT: Franklin Watts, 2003.

May, Suellen. *Invasive Terrestrial Animals*. New York: Chelsea House, 2007.

Taylor, Barbara. *Nature Watch: Snakes*. London, U.K.: Lorenz Books, 2008.

Web Sites

Brown Treesnake Frequently Asked Questions
www.fort.usgs.gov/resources/education/bts/resources/faq.asp
For answers to common questions about this invader

National Invasive Species: Brown Tree Snake
www.invasivespeciesinfo.gov/animals/bts.shtml
For links to recent news articles about and images of this invasive species

North American Brown Tree Snake Control Team
nabtsct.net
To find out about a joint effort between private organizations and federal and state agencies to prevent the brown treesnake from entering the United States

INDEX

ABOUT THE AUTHOR

Barbara A. Somervill writes children's nonfiction books on a variety of topics. She is particularly interested in nature and foreign countries. Somervill believes that researching new and different topics makes writing every book an adventure. When she is not writing, Somervill is an avid reader and plays bridge.